MADAM C. J. WALKER

T0012047

THE BEAUTY BOSS

By Janel Rodríguez

Illustrated by Subi Bosa

Children's Press®
An imprint of Scholastic Inc.

Special thanks to our consultant, A'Lelia Bundles, Madam C. J. Walker's great-great-granddaughter, for her insight into the life and work of Madam C. J. Walker.

Library of Congress Cataloging-in-Publication Data
Names: Rodríguez, Janel, author. | Bosa, Subi, illustrator.
Title: Madam C. J. Walker: The beauty boss / by Janel Rodríguez; illustrated by Subi Bosa.
Description: First edition. | New York, NY: Children's Press, an imprint of Scholastic Inc., 2023. | Series: Bright minds | Includes bibliographical references and index. | Audience: Ages 8–10. | Audience: Grades 4–6. | Summary: "A biography series highlighting the work and social impact of BIPOC inventors"— Provided by publisher.
Identifiers: LCCN 2022028644 (print) | LCCN 2022028645 (ebook) | ISBN 9781338865318 (library binding) | ISBN 9781338865325 (paperback) | ISBN 9781338865332 (ebk)
Subjects: LCSH: Walker, C. J., Madam, 1867–1919—Juvenile literature. | Cosmetics industry—United States—History— Juvenile literature. | African American women executives— Biography—Juvenile literature. | Women millionaires—United States—Biography—Juvenile literature. | BISAC: JUVENILE NONFICTION / Biography & Autobiography / General | JUVENILE FICTION / Technology / Inventions | LCGFT: Biographies.
Classification: LCC HD9970.5.C672 W3576 2023 (print) | LCC HD9970.5.C672 (ebook) | DDC 338.7/66855092 [B]—dc23/ eng/20220708
LC record available at https://lccn.loc.gov/2022028644
LC ebook record available at https://lccn.loc.gov/2022028645

Copyright © 2023 by Scholastic Inc.

All rights reserved. Published by Children's Press, an imprint of Scholastic Inc., *Publishers since 1920*. SCHOLASTIC, CHILDREN'S PRESS, and associated logos are trademarks and/or registered trademarks of Scholastic Inc.

The publisher does not have any control over and does not assume any responsibility for author or third-party websites or their content.

No part of this publication may be reproduced, stored in a retrieval system, or transmitted in any form or by any means, electronic, mechanical, photocopying, recording, or otherwise, without written permission of the publisher. For information regarding permission, write to Scholastic Inc., Attention: Permissions Department, 557 Broadway, New York, NY 10012.

10 9 8 7 6 5 4 3 2 1   23 24 25 26 27

Printed in China   62
First edition, 2023

Book design by Kathleen Petelinsek
Book prototype design by Maria Bergós / Book&Look

Photos ©: cover left: Science History Images/Alamy Images; cover right: Heritage Art/age fotostock; 5 center: Madam C.J. Walker Collection, Indiana Historical Society; 6 top: Madam Walker Family Archives/A'Lelia Bundles; 6 center: David Bohl/Historic New England; 6 map: Elisa Lara/Dreamstime; 7 top: Madam Walker Family Archives/A'Lelia Bundles; 8 bottom: Cci/Shutterstock; 9 top right: Madam C.J. Walker Collection, Indiana Historical Society; 11 bottom center: State Historical Society of Missouri; 14 center: Newspapers. com; 15 bottom right: Science History Images/Alamy Images; 16 center: Everett/Shutterstock; 17 top right: Madam Walker Family Archives/A'Lelia Bundles; 18 center left: Madam Walker Family Archives/A'Lelia Bundles; 18 center right: Heritage Art/age fotostock; 18 bottom center: Heritage Art/age fotostock; 19 center: Madam Walker Family Archives/A'Lelia Bundles; 20 center left: Madam C.J. Walker Collection, Indiana Historical Society; 20 center right: Gado/ Getty Images; 22 center right: Hum Images/Alamy Images; 23 top right: Madam Walker Family Archives/A'Lelia Bundles; 24 all photos: Museum of the City of New York; 25 top: Archive PL/Alamy Images; 25 bottom left: Madam C.J. Walker Collection, Indiana Historical Society; 26 bottom: James Weldon Johnson and Grace Nail Johnson Papers. Yale Collection of American Literature, Beinecke Rare Book and Manuscript Library.; 27 top right: Madam Walker Family Archives/A'Lelia Bundles; 28 center: Dmadeo/Wikimedia; 29 top right: Ed Bailey/AP Images; 29 center: David Bohl/Historic New England; 30 center: Gado/Getty Images; 30 bottom right: Madam Walker Family Archives/A'Lelia Bundles; 31 bottom center: Madam Walker Family Archives/A'Lelia Bundles; 32 center right, 32 bottom left: Raymond Boyd/Michael Ochs Archives/Getty Images; 33 center left: Madam Walker Family Archives/A'Lelia Bundles; 34 center right: Science History Images/Alamy Images; 35 bottom: Google Earth; 40: Author self portrait by Janel Rodriguez.

All other photos © Designed by Freepik and Shutterstock.

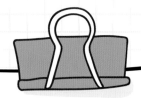

TABLE OF CONTENTS

★ ★ ★ ★

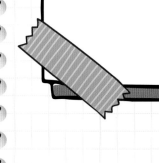
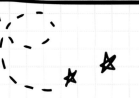

THE RISE OF ...

Before she was the "Beauty Boss," Madam C. J. Walker was a poor orphan girl named Sarah Breedlove. Life was hard for Sarah, but she had dreams of a brighter future.

When I grow up, I'm going to make something of myself and do great things. Just you wait and see!

I made it!

And her dreams came true! Because she worked hard to make them happen for herself.

...SARAH BREEDLOVE

She did it all like a boss—because she *was* one! A proud, respected, and admired leader who developed a very successful line of hair and beauty products and helped thousands of people live better lives.

Hair is power!

Boss

Let's learn more about Sarah—or Madam C. J.—and how her **ambition**, business sense, and concern for the well-being of others made her America's first self-made female millionaire.

IN ESSENCE

Her first home . . .

. . . and her last.

Sarah was born on December 23, 1867, in **Delta, Louisiana**.

She married Moses McWilliams and they had a daughter, **Lelia**.

Sarah died on May 25, 1919 (at age fifty-one), in **Irvington, New York**.

Sarah's daughter later went by the name A'Lelia (pronounced ah-LEEL-ya).

US state map

WASHINGTON
OREGON
MONTANA
NORTH DAKOTA
MINNESOTA
IDAHO
SOUTH DAKOTA
WISCONSIN
WYOMING
MICHIGAN
NEVADA
NEBRASKA
IOWA
UTAH
COLORADO
ILLINOIS
INDIANA
OHIO
PENNSYLVANIA
CALIFORNIA
KANSAS
MISSOURI
WEST VIRGINIA
VIRGINIA
KENTUCKY
ARIZONA
NEW MEXICO
OKLAHOMA
ARKANSAS
TENNESSEE
NORTH CAROLINA
SOUTH CAROLINA
MISSIS-SIPPI
ALABAMA
GEORGIA
TEXAS
LOUISIANA
FLORIDA

NEW HAMPSHIRE
VERMONT
MAINE
NEW YORK
MASSACHUSETTS
RHODE ISLAND
CONNECTICUT
NEW JERSEY
DELAWARE
MARYLAND
WASHINGTON, DC

ALASKA
HAWAII

KNOWN FOR...

- ✅ Inventing a line of hair and beauty products

- ✅ Being an **entrepreneur**

- ✅ Never giving up

- ✅ Employing thousands of Black women

- ✅ Being the boss of a big company with employees all over the United States and beyond

- ✅ Becoming the first *self-made* female millionaire in America

- ✅ Being a generous **philanthropist**

- ✅ Supporting **civil rights**

I got my start by giving myself a start.

Madam C. J. was successful because she took a chance on an idea and believed in herself enough to see it through.

QUOTE:
"I am not ashamed of my past; I am not ashamed of my humble beginnings."

HUMBLE BEGINNINGS

Sarah's parents, Owen and Minerva Breedlove, were born into **slavery** on a plantation in the state of Louisiana. They were forced to work for long hours every day for no pay. Because they were **enslaved**, their children were considered enslaved, too. All except Sarah. By the time she was born, Black people had been declared free.

This one's different.

It's like she knows she's free.

THE END OF SLAVERY IN AMERICA

The Civil War started in the United States in 1861. In it, the Union (the group of states also known as "the North") and the Confederacy (the group of states also known as "the South") battled over slavery. The Union wanted to abolish it. The Confederacy wanted to keep it—even **expand** it. But the Union won the war in 1865. And that same year, the Thirteenth Amendment officially abolished slavery in the United States.

Once free, Sarah's parents became **sharecroppers**. This allowed them to keep or sell some of the crops they harvested. Sadly, this barely improved their living conditions.

By the time Sarah was seven years old, both of her parents had died, leaving her an orphan. When she was ten, she moved to Mississippi to live with her older sister, Louvenia, and her husband.

MISSIS-SIPPI

LOUISIANA

This is a photograph of Sarah as a young woman.

There, instead of going to school, Sarah helped her sister with the hard work of picking cotton.

Unfortunately, Louvenia's husband treated Sarah badly. Sarah wanted to get away from him (and cotton picking) as soon as she could. She married Moses and moved away when she was just fourteen.

When she was seventeen, she became a mother to Lelia.

A PROBLEM PRESENTS ITSELF

In 1887, Sarah's husband Moses died. She now was a nineteen-year-old widow. In search of a better life (again), Sarah decided to move (again). She joined her brothers in St. Louis, Missouri, and found a job washing clothes for $1.50 a week.

In those days, doing laundry was backbreaking work. It required hours of scrubbing clothes with a washboard and bucket.

Life was hard for the poor young mother. Her small home had no running water or electricity. Sarah had very little time to care for her child or herself.

She didn't wash her hair often because she didn't have indoor plumbing. This caused very bad dandruff and scalp infections. Her hair started falling out. It left visible bald patches on her scalp.

Now I have to cover my head, and scarves are just not my style!

LOOKING FOR A CURE

Determined to find a cure for this problem, Sarah **experimented**. She washed her scalp with a mixture of soap products that she used for the laundry. She asked her brothers—who were barbers—for advice.

After trying different **methods** and products, Sarah discovered that a product called "Wonderful Hair Grower" worked best. Even better, it had been created by a Black woman.

WHO WAS ANNIE MALONE?
Annie Malone was the businesswoman whose company made the "Wonderful Hair Grower" Sarah used. Like Sarah, she would go on to become successful, wealthy, and charitable.

★ A BRAND IS BORN ☆

No one knows how Sarah first heard of Annie's hair products. Did she see an ad in the **local** newspaper? Did a salesperson stop by her home? Did a friend recommend them after seeing Sarah struggle with hair loss?

Whatever the reason, Sarah saw working for Annie as a way to better herself. She began selling Annie's products.

Not long after, Sarah moved to Denver, Colorado. There she married a man named Charles Joseph (C. J.) Walker, a newspaper salesman who had moved from St. Louis like her.

HELP!
Throughout her struggles, Sarah was inspired by the example of women from her church. They reached out and helped her when she needed work, tutoring, childcare, and advice. Sarah promised herself that one day, she would be the one helping others, not just the one being helped.

I am now Mrs. C. J. Walker! It has a nice "ring" to it!

In Denver, Sarah continued to sell Annie's products but began dreaming of bigger and better things. Literally.

QUOTE:
"In a dream, a big Black man appeared to me and told me what to mix up for my hair. I made up my mind I would begin to sell it."

To buy those ingredients, she needed money. So she took a second job, as a cook for **pharmacist** Edmund Scholtz.

Some people think Mr. Scholtz told Sarah what ingredients to put in her formula. We'll never know. What we *do* know is that little by little, Sarah bought the ingredients and started experimenting in her "lab" (which was really her attic!).

13

ℬ A DREAM COMES TRUE

Sarah finally made a formula she was happy with. At that point, she stopped working for Annie and began to get her own Wonderful Hair Grower ready to sell. Her husband worked as an "ad man," and he helped her by putting an announcement in the newspaper. Photographs of Sarah were included in the advertisement to help readers quickly recognize her name and face and want to try her product.

QUOTE:
"Having a good article on the market is one thing. Putting it properly before the public is another."

This is one of Sarah's earliest newspaper ads. In it, she modeled her own healthy head of hair.

Mrs. C. J. Walker, hair grower, ...est of many ...through the urgent postponed her ...iends and patrona... and will re- ...tern tour in ...onvince every per- sto... services of her won- derful power of growing hair. One treatment will positively stop the hair from falling out or money refunded. Her treatments have given perfect sat- isfaction to every person in Denver who has given her a trial. She also sells letters of instruction to persons

whom she can not treat personally, teaching them how to grow their own hair at very reasonable prices. With her treatments your hair begins grow- ing at once. A trial treatment will convince you. Two years ago her hair was less than a finger's length. This is the result of only two years' treat- ment. Persons out of town wishing letters of instruction, with her won- derful grower, can address her at 2410 Champa, 'phone Pink 592.

She is referred to as **"Mrs. C. J. Walker"** here. Not long after their marriage, Sarah changed her name and used the more dignified title of **"Madam C. J. Walker"** instead.

"Madam" sounded French. Paris, the capital of France, was the world capital of beauty. This made her new name sound even better!

Little by little, Madam C. J. introduced new products to her line. She had learned that the most effective way to market them was to demonstrate how to use them. Sometimes she did so by washing and styling her own hair in front of potential customers. Other times she washed and styled theirs—for free! Either way, the results spoke for themselves. Soon orders started pouring in.

When she made enough money, Madam C. J. opened a beauty salon where women could get their hair done using only her products. She also trained hairdressers and other salespeople (whom she called "agents") to work for her.

Some of her hair products came in small, round tins with her picture on the cover (like this one).

RIVALRY AND INSPIRATION

When Annie Malone heard about Madam C. J.'s success, she accused her of "stealing" her formula. But Madam C. J. did not have the same exact formula as Annie. Also, some people think Madam C. J. copied the name "Wonderful Hair Grower" from Annie, but this phrase had been used to sell hair products before either of them.

However, it is undeniable that Madam C. J. was inspired by Annie. When she saw what a Black lady could accomplish through hard work and the right attitude, she knew she could do it, too—only in her own way. And both women were very successful.

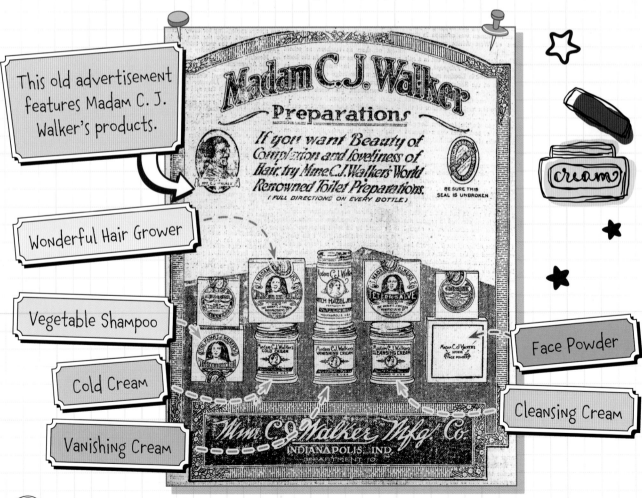

This old advertisement features Madam C. J. Walker's products.

Wonderful Hair Grower

Vegetable Shampoo

Cold Cream

Vanishing Cream

Face Powder

Cleansing Cream

In 1906, Madam C. J. left her daughter in charge of the office in Denver and began traveling the United States. Everywhere she went, she advertised in newspapers and taught classes in hair care. She wanted as many Black women as possible to know about and use her products.

In 1908, Madam C. J. opened a school in Pittsburgh, Pennsylvania. She named it The Lelia College of Beauty Culturists. She would name all her schools after her daughter.

In 1906, Lelia was in her early twenties, married, and old enough to help her mother run the company.

2337
The Lelia College
of Beauty Culturists
Mme. C. J Walker
NOW OPEN

Agriculturists grow plants. We, beauty culturists, grow hair. And teach women how to care for it.

THE WALKER SYSTEM

Sales agents for Madam C. J. went through a several-week training course in hair care before selling Walker products. They were taught how to best use the products so that they could then show customers.

This was called the "Walker System." And after seeing good results, many customers would become agents, too.

A class of Walker sales agents

AUTHORIZED AGENT
Wm. C. J. Walker's
SYSTEM AND PREPARATIONS

Madam C. J. is sitting in the middle.

Graduates of Lelia College would receive certificates like this one.

The Lelia College
Indianapolis, Indiana
For Teaching Mme. C. J. Walkers' Method of Growing Hair
This Certifies That

INDEPENDENCE FOR WOMEN

Because of racial **discrimination**, most Black women could only get housekeeping or farm-working jobs. These jobs did not pay well. But Walker agents were paid very well! This was because Madam C. J. didn't only want to make money for herself. She wanted to help other Black women make money, too.

Walker agents made more money in a week than most Black women who worked as maids made in a month.

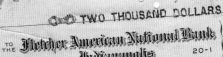

The Mme. C. J. Walker Mfg. Co.   No. 1857
INCORPORATED
640 N. WEST STREET

THE FLETCHER AMERICAN NATIONAL BANK OF INDIANAPOLIS

Indianapolis July 2 1915 $2000

Pay to the order of   F. J. Ransom   Dollars

TWO THOUSAND DOLLARS   THE MME. C. J. WALKER MFG. CO. INC.

TO THE Fletcher American National Bank
Indianapolis   20-1   BY Mme. C. J. Walker PRESIDENT

A check with the signature of Madam C. J.

BLACK BEAUTY

Before companies like Madam C. J.'s existed, beauty products were made mainly for white women. Black women had to make their own. And when they were enslaved, lack of time and money made this more difficult. Still, Black women not only managed to beautify themselves, but they also helped one another do so. With her company, Madam C. J. was following this tradition of Black women helping Black women, only on a larger scale.

★ MADAM C. J. WALKER INC.

Madam C. J. was soon famous! Black women all over the country now knew about, bought, and used her products. Her sales went up and up. Her business boomed.

In 1910, she settled in Indianapolis, Indiana. Behind her home, she had a lab and a **factory** built to manufacture her products, as well as a salon and beauty school.

Madam C. J. Walker stands at the entrance of her impressive Indianapolis home.

Before the year was over, she **employed** close to 1,000 beauty culturists. Thousands of women enjoyed being styled and **pampered** in her salon. And thousands more ordered products from the office and from her sales agents. The products were mailed to customers' homes all over the country.

All of Walker's products that were manufactured in this factory bore the words "Made by the Madam C. J. Walker Manufacturing Co., Indianapolis, Ind."

Madam C. J.'s offices in Indiana were a busy place!

LADY BOUNTIFUL

As Madam C. J.'s fame grew, she became known for being very rich and very generous. Some examples of her generosity are:

- ☑ She held a **fundraiser** to buy a harp for a young woman studying music.

- ☑ She contributed to a fund for an ambulance for Black soldiers in France during World War I.

- ☑ She donated money to an orphanage.

- ☑ She paid **tuition** for students to attend Tuskegee Institute, the college for Black excellence headed by educator and author **Booker T. Washington**.

- ☑ Madam C. J. even gave away forty Christmas dinners to struggling families.

WHO WAS BOOKER T. WASHINGTON?

Booker T. Washington was one of the most influential Black Americans at the time. In 1912, Madam C. J. attended a business conference that he organized. There she wished to give a speech, but Booker T. would not call her to the stage. So she stood up and addressed everyone from her place in the audience. She spoke so well that he invited her back as an official speaker the following year.

> Thank you so much. I promise to help someone else.

> Thank you! That is what I was hoping you would do! Merry Christmas!

When she donated $1,000 to open a **YMCA** (community space and gymnasium) for Black men and boys, people were shocked. "How could a woman—let alone a Black one—have that much money to give away?" they wondered. "Could she really be that rich?"

A newspaper reporter visited her and said she was indeed that rich, and described a "golden room" in her home. Its furnishings included gold chairs, an oriental rug, oil paintings, and a **Victrola** painted in gold leaf!

Madam C. J. with **Booker T. Washington** at the opening of the new Black YMCA in Indiana.

Wow! She really is the boss around here!

NEW YORK, NEW YORK

After six years of marriage, the Walkers divorced. The following year, in 1913, Madam C. J. traveled to the Caribbean and Central America to expand her business. This gave her brand **international** recognition.

Meanwhile, Lelia moved to New York City. She hired **architect** Vertner Tandy to redesign her **townhouse**.

Their new home stood on West 136th Street in Harlem.

Lelia lived on the top floors.

The second floor was a Lelia College beauty school.

There isn't any place else like it!

I'm going to throw a lot of great parties here!

The first floor was a Madam C. J. Walker beauty salon.

WHO WAS VERTNER TANDY?

Vertner Tandy was possibly the first registered Black architect in New York State and the first to open his own business in New York City. Some of his most famous works have been **designated** national **landmarks**.

When the townhouse was complete, both mother and daughter were very pleased. So pleased, in fact, that in 1916, Madam C. J. hired **Mr. Tandy** to design a new home for her in Irvington, New York.

The mansion would take two years to complete.

In the meantime, Madam C. J. decided to put her trustworthy lawyer, **Freeman B. Ransom**, in charge of the office in Indiana so she could move in with Lelia and run her company from New York City.

F. B. Ransom was an excellent lawyer who became a friend to both Madam C. J. and Lelia.

25

GETTING INVOLVED

While living in the city, Madam C. J. became more involved with fighting prejudice. She joined the **NAACP** and brainstormed with Black leaders, such as Ida B. Wells, Mary McLeod Bethune, and W. E. B. Du Bois, different ways to combat **racism**. She also traveled to different states to give speeches and donated money to groups that promoted racial equality.

This is the greatest country under the sun, but we must not let our love for it stop us from protesting against wrong and injustice.

WHAT IS THE NAACP?

The NAACP (National Association for the Advancement of Colored People) was founded in 1909 by both Black and white people. Its aim was to raise awareness of racial discrimination and violence. It wanted to put an end to this discrimination in all areas of life, including schools, the workplace, public spaces, housing, and government.

In 1917, Madam C. J. and about 10,000 other people participated in a silent march down Fifth Avenue. It was one of the first mass civil rights protests led by a national organization. A few days later, she traveled with a group to Washington, DC. The group asked lawmakers to protect the rights of Black people.

Black women, men, and children all took part in the Silent Protest Parade of 1917.

LEADING THE WAY

By 1917, there were thousands of saleswomen working for Madam C. J. spread out all over the country. She organized them into local chapters and held a **convention** in Philadelphia, Pennsylvania.

About 400 agents attended. It was one of the first **national** meetings of businesswomen in the United States. There Madam C. J. gave away prizes to those who sold the most products *and* those who gave away the most to charity!

Walker agents who attended the first national convention in 1917

you're both the best!

She also wanted them to pay attention to civil rights. At the end of the convention, the delegates sent a telegram to President Woodrow Wilson urging him to support laws to protect Black people.

VILLA LEWARO

Madam C. J.'s new home was ready in 1918. It was a **showplace** of terraces, marble floors, and chandeliers. Live-in servants were employed to look after its thirty-four rooms. They included a library and a gymnasium. There was even an organ that, thanks to specially built "**ducts**" in the walls, could actually "pipe" music into rooms throughout the house.

It was a palace on the Hudson River!

Many of Madam C. J.'s neighbors were famous millionaires. They had last names such as Vanderbilt, Rockefeller, and Roosevelt.

Madam C. J. wanted her new home to be built close to the road so that it could be seen and admired by passersby.

And now my dreams have come true!

After having worked so hard all her life, Madam C. J. wanted her home to be a place of rest. But she also wanted it to be an inspiration to other Black people. She hoped it would show them that it was possible for them to succeed at business and become leaders in their communities, too.

People sailing up and down the Hudson River could also admire Madam C. J.'s new home from the back.

VILLA LEWARO
Seeing Madam C. J.'s mansion for the first time, opera singer Enrico Caruso said it looked like an Italian "villa" (a large country estate). So Madam C. J. named it Villa Lewaro. And what does "Lewaro" mean? It's a made-up word from the first two letters of her daughter's name: **LE**lia **WA**lker **RO**binson. (John Robinson was Lelia's first husband.)

DEATH OF A SALESWOMAN

By the time she was fifty-one years old, Madam C. J. had several health problems. Her doctors told her to stay home, rest, and enjoy her beautiful mansion. But Madam C. J. found it hard to stay still.

While on a speaking tour of St. Louis, Missouri, she became sick and had to be sent home. She died a month later, on May 25, 1919.

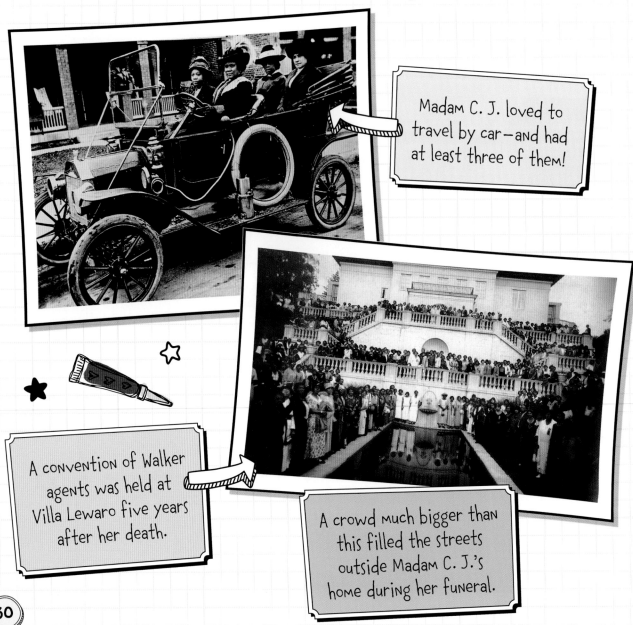

Madam C. J. loved to travel by car—and had at least three of them!

A convention of Walker agents was held at Villa Lewaro five years after her death.

A crowd much bigger than this filled the streets outside Madam C. J.'s home during her funeral.

At her death, Madam C. J.'s fortune, home, and company combined were valued to be worth **one million dollars**.

In her will, she left one-third of her money to her daughter and about two-thirds to charities.

ONE MILLION DOLLARS

IN NUMBERS
During her lifetime, Madam C. J. contributed more than $125,000—or about $2 million in today's dollars—to schools, YMCAs, churches, orphanages, arts organizations, community groups, and political causes.

That's about $17 million today!

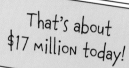

Lelia became the new boss of the Madam C. J. Walker Manufacturing Company.

LEGACY OF A LIFE WELL LIVED

After Madam C. J.'s death, the Walker Company moved its Indianapolis headquarters to a much larger, four-story building. It included not only the factory, salon, and beauty school, but also a Black-owned barbershop, restaurant, ballroom, drugstore, and doctor's office. Most impressive of all was the **grand movie theater**. It played first-run movies and featured Black entertainers and performers.

What a tribute to Madam C. J. Walker!

The building still stands today on Indiana Avenue. It is known as the Madam Walker Legacy Center and is a National Historic Landmark. It continues the legacy of Madam C. J.

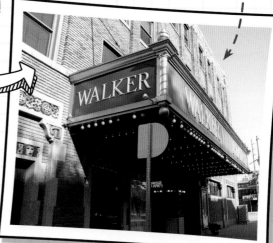

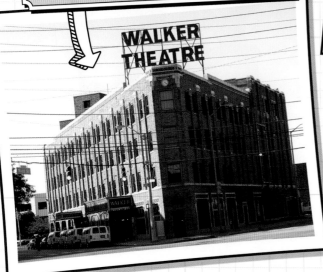

In 1998, the United States Postal Service honored Madam C. J. with an official **postage stamp** with her photo on it.

And although the building in Harlem where Madam C. J. and Lelia once lived was torn down long ago, the street where it stood was **named after them**.

Madam C. J. Walker's life was difficult at first. But she worked hard to make her dreams come true and help others. Today, more than one hundred years after her death, Madam C. J. Walker is still remembered for her hard work, determination, and generosity.

MODERN PRODUCTS

In 2022, Madam C. J.'s products were continued with a hair-care line called MADAM by Madam C. J. Walker, sold exclusively at Walmart. It features many modern hair products such as curl creams, leave-in conditioners, shampoos, and scalp serums. They were all inspired by the original spirit of the "Beauty Boss."

And the most important thing she would want you to learn from reading about her life is . . .

QUOTE:
"What I have done, you can do!"

YOUR TURN!

Madam C. J. used to travel across America and share her success story. She would tell her listeners, "I am here to interest and inspire you." She wanted her story to give others hope and to spark their creativity. How has learning about her inspired you? Pick one of these three activities to help you think about this!

You, the Business Person

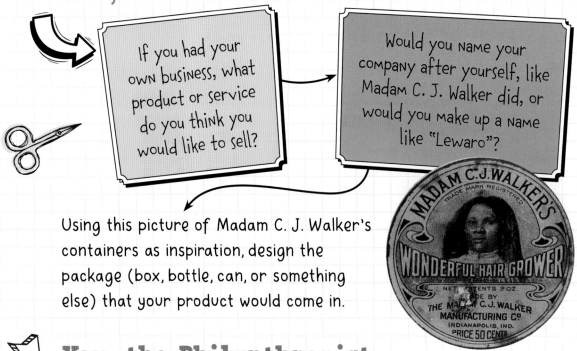

If you had your own business, what product or service do you think you would like to sell?

Would you name your company after yourself, like Madam C. J. Walker did, or would you make up a name like "Lewaro"?

Using this picture of Madam C. J. Walker's containers as inspiration, design the package (box, bottle, can, or something else) that your product would come in.

You, the Philanthropist

If you were very rich, what causes or charities would you donate money to?

Who or what would you help if you could?

The homeless?

Animal shelters?

Space travel?

Do some research and list as many organizations, ideas, or people as you want.

...And Just for Fun

What if you got to build your own dream house?

What would you want it to look like? How big would it be? Would it be in the country or city? How many rooms would it have?

Would you have friends or family living with you?

Would you have a pool in your dream home, like Villa Lewaro?

Write an essay about it.

Let your imagination run wild!

GLOSSARY

ambition (am-BISH-uhn) something that you want to do in the future; a strong wish to be successful

architect (AHR-ki-tekt) someone who designs buildings and supervises the way they are built

civil rights (SIV-uhl rites) the individual rights that all members of a democratic society have to freedom and equal treatment under the law

convention (kuhn-VEN-shuhn) a formal gathering of people who have the same profession or interests

designated (DEZ-ig-nay-ted) to have named or marked something

discrimination (dis-krim-i-NAY-shuhn) prejudice or unfair behavior toward others based on differences in such things as age, race, or gender

ducts (duhkts) tubes that carry air or liquid from one place to another

employed (em-PLOID) to have paid someone to do work

enslaved (en-SLAYVD) unfair condition of being owned by another person

entrepreneur (ahn-truh-pruh-NUR) someone who starts businesses and finds new ways to make money

expand (ik-SPAND) to become larger

experimented (ik-SPER-uh-ment-ed) to have scientifically tested or tried something in order to learn something particular

fundraiser (FUHND-ray-zer) an event to raise money for a cause or charity

international (in-tur-NASH-uh-nuhl) involving more than one country, as in international banking

landmarks (LAND-mahrks) buildings or places selected and pointed out as important

local (LOH-kuhl) of or having to do with the area in which you live

methods (METH-uhds) particular ways of doing something

national (NASH-uh-nuhl) of, having to do with, or shared by a whole nation

pampered (PAM-purd) to have taken very good care of yourself or someone else with food, kindness, or anything special

pharmacist (FAHR-muh-sist) a person who is trained to prepare and dispense drugs and medicines

philanthropist (fuh-LAN-thruh-pist) a person who helps others by giving time or money to causes and charities

racism (RAY-si-zuhm) the belief that a particular race is better than others; treating people unfairly or cruelly because of their race

sharecroppers (SHAIR-krah-purz) farmers who work land for the owner in return for a share of the value of the crop

showplace (SHOW-plase) a place of beauty or interest that attracts many visitors

slavery (SLAY-vur-ee) unfair condition in which one human being is owned by another

tuition (too-ISH-uhn) money paid to a college or private school in order for a student to study there

Victrola (vik-TROH-la) an early brand of record player typically used for playing large discs of music

YMCA (why-em-see-ay) an international organization that promotes the spiritual, intellectual, social, and physical welfare of originally young Christian men

INDEX

FURTHER READING

Black, Donnette. *Madam C. J. Walker's Road to Success*. Bloomington, IN: Author House, 2010.

Bundles, A'Lelia. *All about Madam C. J. Walker*. Indianapolis, IN: Blue River Press, 2020.

Lasky, Kathryn. Illustrated by Nneka Bennett. *Vision of Beauty: The Story of Sarah Breedlove Walker*. Somerville, MA: Candlewick Press, 2012.

Lee, Sally. *Madam C. J. Walker: The Woman behind Hair Care Products for African Americans*. North Mankato, MN: Pebble, 2019.

McAneney, Caitie. *Madam C. J. Walker and Her Beauty Empire*. New York: PowerKids Press, 2016.

Read the other books in this series:

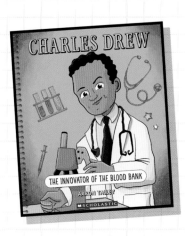

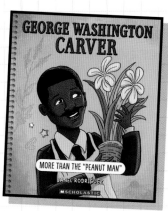

ABOUT THE AUTHOR

Janel Rodríguez is a "Nuyorican"—that is, a Puerto Rican who was born and raised in New York City. She wrote the book *Super SHEroes of History: Civil Rights* for Scholastic. Like Madam C. J., she is very interested in hair care and has had fun experimenting with different styles, colors, and treatments over the years. (These days she's trying life as a blonde!)

ABOUT THE ILLUSTRATOR

As a child, Subi Bosa drew pictures all the time, in every room of the house—sometimes even on the walls! His mother always told everyone, "He knew how to draw before he could properly hold a pencil." Today, Subi continues to draw fun picture books, comics, and graphic novels from his home in Cape Town, a city in South Africa. He has won many awards for his work!